essentials

Planning Your Retirement

Time-saving books that teach specific skills to busy people, focusing on what really matters; the things that make a difference – the *essentials*. Other books in the series include:

Selling Your Home Using Feng Shui

Writing Good Reports

Speaking in Public

Responding to Stress

Succeeding at Interviews

Solving Problems

Hiring People

Getting Started on the Internet

Writing Great Copy

Making the Best Man's Speech

Making Great Presentations

Making the Most of Your Time

For full details please send for a free copy of the latest catalogue. See back cover for address.

The things that really matter about

Planning
Your
Retirement

John Humphries

ESSENTIALS

Published in 2000 by
How To Books Ltd, 3 Newtec Place,
Magdalen Road, Oxford OX4 1RE, United Kingdom
Tel: (01865) 793806   Fax: (01865) 248780
email: info@howtobooks.co.uk
www.howtobooks.co.uk

British Library Cataloguing in Publication Data.
A catalogue record for this book is available from
the British Library.

Edited by Diana Brueton
Cover design by Shireen Nathoo Design
Cover copy by Sallyann Sheridan
Produced for How To Books by Deer Park Productions
Typeset by PDQ Typesetting, Newcastle-under-Lyme, Staffordshire
Printed and bound by Hillman Printers, Frome, Somerset.

NOTE: The material contained in this book is set out in good faith for
general guidance and no liability can be accepted for loss or expense
incurred as a result of relying in particular circumstances on
statements made in the book. Laws and regulations are complex
and liable to change, and readers should check the current position
with the relevant authorities before making personal arrangements.

ESSENTIALS *is an imprint of*
How To Books

Contents

Preface

When you retire you will be starting a new phase in your life. It should be the time to relax and enjoy yourself. However, retirement may also prompt a number of questions such as: What can I do with my time? Should I move home? How can I make sure I have enough money? What benefits am I entitled to? What happens to my estate when my retirement comes to an end as unfortunately it inevitably will?

Hopefully these and many other questions are answered in this book. So please read it, use the information and have a long and happy retirement.

John Humphries

1 Changing Gear

The message is to approach retirement with a positive attitude.

4

things that
really matter

1 **ADAPTING TO CHANGE**

2 **MAKING THE MOST OF YOUR TIME**

3 **LEARNING TO RELAX**

4 **KEEPING HEALTHY**
°

Whilst many people look forward to their retirement with eager anticipation, others dread the prospect. The main reason why some people fear retirement is because they have made no plans or preparation for what after all should be **the most interesting and exciting phase of their lives**.

The retirement age in the United Kingdom is traditionally 65 for men and 60 for women to coincide with their entitlement to receive a state pension, although this will be equalised to 65 for both sexes in 2020. However, an increasing number of people are opting to retire earlier, either through personal choice or their employer's policy.

Retirement will mean many changes to your lifestyle. It is important to **recognise and adapt to these changes** as quickly as possible to avoid the possibility of stress. You will have much more time on your hands and it is vital to use this time to **enjoy your retirement**. As we get older we tend to worry more about our health, so it is important to maintain as healthy a lifestyle as possible.

IS THIS YOU?

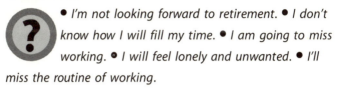

• I'm not looking forward to retirement. • I don't know how I will fill my time. • I am going to miss working. • I will feel lonely and unwanted. • I'll miss the routine of working.

① ADAPTING TO CHANGE

Regardless of the age at which you retire, it will result in a number of **changes to your life**. Here are some of the main changes together with suggestions on how to adapt.

- If you are married, you and your partner will spend much more time together, which can prove stressful. Agree to share the household chores; choose separate activities so that you spend time apart and have more to talk about.
- Feeling lonely. Single people often dread the thought of having to spend more time on their own. There are many clubs and societies which people can join to meet others with similar interests. Most libraries have details of these organisations.
- You will no longer have set routines such as getting up at specific times, travelling to work and taking lunch at times determined by your employer. If you miss such routines, set some for yourself. Walk to the newsagent each morning to buy your newspaper; undertake activities such as shopping, exercising and housework at pre-planned times each day or week.
- Loss of stimulation. Keep your mind active by reading, doing crosswords and making the effort to meet and talk with other people.
- Feeling not needed any more. Unfortunately many people believe that once they have retired they can no longer contribute anything to society. This is far from the

case. There are many opportunities for such people to use their skills and experience for the benefit of others, voluntary work being the most obvious.

Being retired means that you can be more flexible. No longer will you have to confine your gardening, decorating or shopping to weekends or evenings. You can take your holidays when you wish, not when your employer says you can.

Within reason you can now do what you like when you like.

 MAKING THE MOST OF YOUR TIME

Although some people have planned how they will spend their retirement almost to the minute, the majority have little idea how they will fill their time beyond decorating the house, keeping the garden tidy and perhaps taking a holiday. As a result such people quickly become bored, which can also lead to stress.

There is now no excuse for letting this new-found free time simply slip by. There are more opportunities to **enjoy this time and have a fulfilled life** than ever before. So let's look at some of these options and, if you have not already decided what to do, it will give you some ideas to explore.

Working

There are several reasons to keep working after you have retired. This is the chance to

- try something new
- keep your mind and body active
- give something back to the community
- or perhaps the extra income will be useful.

If you are unsure as to the type of work that would suit you, do a **SWOT analysis** on yourself. This is a technique used by many companies to determine their **strengths**, **weaknesses**, **opportunities** and **threats**. First list all your strengths: all your skills such as driving, speaking a foreign language, keyboard skills, playing the piano and so on. Then write down your weaknesses: this is more difficult so be honest. Your list might include such things as lack of computer skills, selling, unable to drive etc. Next come opportunities: look at the local papers for jobs where your strengths could be used and your weaknesses would have no effect. Finally consider any threats such as age, physical disabilities, travelling and hours to be worked. When you have located suitable employment, it is very important that you must want to do it and enjoy it – after all, it is your choice.

- **Full- and part-time employment**. Opportunities include shop assistants, van driving, clerical work, delivering directories, mail shots and newspapers, delivering and collecting for mail order companies and local tourist guides. SAGA and Eurocamp often have requirements for mature couriers and holiday reps.
- **Homeworking**. Several companies offer work that people can do in their own homes. The type of work is quite varied, such as light assembly work, clerical, mailing, craftwork and market research. Details of agencies handling this work can often be found in newsagents' windows. However, be warned, the money offered is usually quite low.
- **Self-employed**. This is the chance to earn from your interest and hobbies. If you have skills such as woodworking, toy-making, needlecraft, picture framing or any other craft, you may wish to sell the items you

make. This can best be done through mail order, car boot sales and small craft fairs. Or you may possess knowledge and skills which you can offer to companies on a freelance, consultancy basis. Many retired people have established very successful businesses by identifying a niche market for their skills such as local tourist guides, stylish clothes for the older person and alternative health clinics.

If you decide to set up a business there are a few points to consider:

– You may have to pay tax on your income.

– Don't invest large sums of money on equipment or premises until you are certain that the business will be successful.

– Do enough people want your particular skill or what you produce?

– Take advice from your local Training and Enterprise Council; many run courses in starting up a business.

- **Voluntary work**. Volunteers are always needed and welcomed by a wide variety of charities and organisations.

  – Charities: fundraisers, organisers, shop assistants, drivers, collectors.

  – National Trust and English Heritage: guides and helpers.

  – Nature reserves: guides and helpers.

  – Political parties: all types of help.

  – Hospitals: driving patients to and from hospital.

  – Primary schools: teacher assistants, particularly for reading.

  – Youth work: scouts, guides and youth clubs usually welcome outside help.

Voluntary work can be very rewarding but beware of becoming 'too willing a horse' or you will find that you have no time for anything else.

Leisure activities

You may already have a number of hobbies to which you can now devote more of your time. On the other hand this is your chance to **try those things that you have always wanted to do** but have never had the time. There are literally hundreds of different activities available so let's look at some of them.

- **Gardening** – start planning for the time when you may not be as active as you are now by building raised flower beds, planting easily maintained shrubs and bushes, making paths and patios.
- **DIY** – build those long-wanted shelves, decorate inside and out, replace the guttering.
- **Music** – learn to play an instrument, join a local choral society.
- **Dancing** – old time, ballroom, line dancing, salsa, English, Irish and Scottish folk dancing. Most of these are available locally.
- **Drama** – strut your stuff on stage or help behind the scenes at your local amateur dramatic or operatic society.
- **Reading** – catch up on all those books you have wanted to read.
- **Writing** – try writing short stories, poems, articles of local interest, you might get them published. Keep a detailed diary.
- **Crafts** – painting, pottery, needlework, weaving, photography, model making, woodwork.

- **Genealogy** – trace your family history.
- **Travel** – this is the chance to visit all those places you have been meaning to go to, within your financial means, now you don't have to travel during peak times. If you are single, Travel Companions (see Useful Addresses) can arrange for you to take holidays with a suitable companion.
- **Sport** – there are many sports suitable for older people even if you have not tried them before such as:
  – bowls: with the introduction of indoor rinks, this can be played all year round
  – golf: good exercise and you do not have to be a good player to enjoy it
  – badminton: a sociable game played at all levels
  – tennis: similar benefits to badminton
  – archery: you do not need to be particularly fit to enjoy it
  – snooker: although the professionals are getting younger, it is still an enjoyable game for the older person
  – coaching: if you have played soccer, rugby, cricket or other such team sports, local clubs welcome coaches for their younger players.
  Other sporting activities are included in the section below on keeping healthy. Even though you may feel fit, it is not wise to take up a strenuous sport such as squash at a late age.

Other activities

- **House-sitting** – looking after a family's home while they are away. This gives you the chance to stay in other parts of the country and receive a small payment.

- **Pet care** – The Cinnamon Trust (see Useful Addresses) seeks people to look after other people's pets while they are on holiday.
- **The Dark Horse Venture** offers you the chance to discover your hidden talents and try new challenges.

Increasing your knowledge

It is never too late to learn. There is an ever-increasing opportunity for retired people to learn new skills.

Adult Education. Most local authorities run classes in a wide range of subjects from computer appreciation, conversational French, GCSE and A level subjects and local history to cake decorating, water colour painting and feng shui. Many classes are held during the daytime and details will be available from your local library.

Open University. Why not study at home for a degree in a subject which interests you?

Open College of Arts offers home-based courses in subjects such as sculpture, garden design, textiles and creative writing.

The University of the Third Age provides educational and leisure activities for older people at their local branches.

Correspondence courses are available in a range of subjects such as writing, proof-reading and alternative therapies and are usually advertised in newspapers.

Here are a few more activities which you may like to pursue:

- The Ugly Model Agency needs people to model clothes for the older person for magazines and catalogues.
- The Cinnamon Trust requires people to foster pets whilst their owners are in hospital or on holiday.

- The Oral History Society wants people to record the memories of older people for school projects and historical research.
- Travel Companions offers a travel companion matching service for people up to the age of 75.
- The Dark Horse Venture invites retired people to discover their hidden talents.
- The Running Sixties welcomes people over 60 to start running and you don't have to be ultra-fit or a regular runner to join.

 LEARNING TO RELAX

We live in a world of ever-increasing pressures which affect all of us, even in retirement. It is therefore important that we learn to relax. This may seem obvious, but do we take time to really relax and do we know how to?

Several simple exercises which you can practise will help you to overcome the everyday tensions and stresses.

Deep breathing

- Make yourself comfortable either sitting, standing or lying down.
- Keep your back straight.
- Breathe in slowly through your nose.
- Hold your breath for five seconds.
- Breathe out slowly through your mouth.
- Repeat this two or three times.

Relaxing your body

- Sit comfortably in a chair.
- Begin by deep breathing.
- Turn your thoughts to each part of your body in turn.

- Starting with your left foot, relax it until it feels heavy, then your right foot.
- Next comes each leg in turn followed by the back and spine, remember to breathe gently and easily each time.
- Relax your stomach and chest, then each arm and hand.
- Keep each part of your body fully relaxed before moving on.
- Then relax your shoulders and neck.
- When relaxing your face, close your eyes, let your tongue drop to the bottom of your mouth and put your lips lightly together.
- Let your mind wander and think 'happy thoughts'.
- Slowly wiggle your hands and feet, open your eyes and sit quietly until you are ready to move. You should now feel completely relaxed.

Relaxing your mind

- Sit comfortably and close your eyes.
- Now use your imagination. Picture a beautiful flower or scene. Let the image fade, then bring it back. Change the colours in your mind's eye.
- Imagine space between your eyes, between your ears and in your mouth.
- Allow one arm to feel heavier than the other.
- Imagine you are floating in a warm bath.
- Feel the weight of your body in the chair.
- When your mind is totally relaxed sit quietly before opening your eyes.

Yoga

This is a Hindu discipline originally designed to train the mind to reach a state of spiritual insight and tranquility. It is also an excellent way of relaxing both mind and body. Before attempting to practise it at home, it is advisable to attend classes to learn the technique. Most local authorities offer tuition.

Other techniques

There are a number of tapes and CDs on the market which are designed to help you relax with sounds such as waves lapping on the shore, wind rustling in the trees, bird songs, the sounds of whales and dolphins calling to each other and gentle, rhythmic music. Sit quietly, listen to the sounds and clear your mind of all other thoughts and you will feel more relaxed.

 KEEPING HEALTHY

As we get older, we naturally tend to worry more about our health.

It is very important that we take responsibility to keep ourselves as healthy as possible.

The best ways to keep healthy are through **regular exercise** and a **sensible diet**.

Exercise

Everyone can take part in some form of exercise regardless of age or physical fitness. There are good reasons for taking regular exercise, it:

- reduces the risk of coronary heart disease
- helps control blood pressure and mild hypertension
- increases stamina
- helps prevent brittle bone disease
- improves muscle strength and joint flexibility

– helps to reduce stress

– increases your energy levels

– helps to reduce obesity-related diseases

– will help improve your sex life

– will make you feel much better.

So what can we do?

- **Walking**. The easiest and among the best forms of exercise. A brisk 20-minute walk four times a week will help to keep you fit.

- **Jogging**. A popular exercise with many people but take care as it can damage the joints.

- **Cycling**. This combines exercise and visiting different places. It can be undertaken at your own pace and now that several thousand miles of cycle ways are being opened up you can ride well away from motor traffic, making it much safer.

- **Swimming**. A 30-minute swim once or twice a week will help to keep your muscles toned and your joints flexible. Most swimming pools have sessions for the over-60s. If you cannot swim, classes are usually available.

- **Keep fit**. The majority of leisure centres run keep fit sessions for the older person. These are usually at different levels to satisfy individual levels of fitness. Before joining a keep fit class, you will normally be asked to take a 'fitness assessment' to determine the most suitable exercises for you. A few gentle exercises each morning when you get out of bed can be very beneficial.

Other activities include gardening, golf and tennis which help to improve and maintain your fitness and health.

It is important to take forms of exercise which you enjoy and can do regularly without over-stretching yourself.

Remember that pulled muscles and ligament problems take longer to heal the older you get.

Diet

There is much publicity about keeping to a healthy diet and there is a wide range of ready meals and other foods available to meet these requirements. Unfortunately they tend to be more expensive than other foods. However, it is not necessary to spend more money to keep to a good, healthy diet. Here are a few suggestions:

- Buy semi-skimmed milk, fresh fruit and vegetables, fish such as tinned tuna, fresh herring and mackerel, wholemeal bread, chicken, lamb's liver, low fat margarine and yoghurt, eggs and tins of baked beans.
- Reduce the amount of meat per portion and bulk up with vegetables and pulses. Three or four ounces of meat per portion is normally sufficient.
- Use recipes to keep your meals interesting and varied.
- Make sure your meals contain sufficient vitamins and minerals:
  Vitamin D: oily fish, eggs, margarine and some yoghurts
  Vitamin C: citrus fruit, blackcurrants, tomatoes and green vegetables
  Calcium: milk, cheese, nuts, pulses and bread
  Iron: lean red meat, liver, pulses and dark green vegetables
  Zinc: lean meat, wholewheat foods and pulses
  Potassium: bananas

These can also be taken in the form of tablets to supplement your diet.

- Drink plenty of water, flavoured or plain, six to eight

glasses a day.

- Cut down on the alcohol, although a glass of red wine a day will help to keep the blood flowing.
- Garlic capsules are good for the heart and circulation.

Being retired you now have more time to plan and prepare nourishing, healthy meals.

MAKING WHAT MATTERS WORK FOR YOU

✓ Develop a positive attitude towards retirement. You have earned it, so enjoy it.

✓ Plan your time so that you have events to look forward to. Decide what type of activities you want to do and find out from newspapers, libraries etc what is available locally. Try things you have never done before and make the effort to meet people and enlarge your social circle.

✓ Take the time to relax properly once a day.

✓ Exercise regularly and sensibly and eat a healthy diet.

2 Getting Your Entitlements

Upon reaching the state retirement age, the majority of people in the UK will be entitled to receive a state pension.

5 things that really matter

1 **STATE RETIREMENT PENSION**

2 **INCREASING YOUR STATE PENSION**

3 **COMPANY AND PRIVATE PENSIONS**

4 **ADDITIONAL STATE BENEFITS**

5 **CONCESSIONS**

As well as the state pension there are many other benefits to which you may be entitled, depending upon your circumstances. The purpose of this chapter is to make you aware of these benefits so that you can ensure you receive everything that is due to you.

All state pensions and other benefits are dealt with by the Benefit Agency whose head office is in Newcastle upon Tyne and branches throughout the country. **It is in each individual's interest to make sure that they are receiving everything that is due to them**. Whilst this chapter attempts to provide as much general information as possible, if you require further details, apply to the Benefit Agency for booklet NP46.

If you have a company or personal pension, it is your responsibility to make sure that you receive all that you are entitled to from it. In addition there are numerous other concessions designed to save you money.

IS THIS YOU?

● *I'll only have my state pension to live on.* ● *I don't know what I'm entitled to.* ● *Will I have to pay tax on my pension?* ● *Where can I get help?* ● *What can I do to save money?*

STATE RETIREMENT PENSION

Upon reaching pension age, the majority of citizens in the country will be entitled to receive a state pension. Currently the pension age is 65 for men and 60 for women. However, the Pensions Act 1995 will change the women's pension age to 65 by 2020.

How much will I get?

The amount of the pension is determined by the government. The actual amount that you will receive depends upon the number of years you have paid NI contributions, these are known as **qualifying years**. To receive the full 100% pension you must have qualifying years of 90% of your working life. Thus if your working life is 41 years or more, you need 36 qualifying years. If you have worked for say 35 years, but only have 20 qualifying years, you will receive 65% of the basic pension.

For calculation purposes, **working life** is said to commence at 18. If you spent time doing National Service, although you would not have made any NI contributions you will be credited with those years. Unfortunately this is not the case for time spent at university or in other higher education. Four months before reaching the state retirement age you will be sent form BR1 which will detail what is due to you. You can request a **pension forecast** at any time before you retire by applying for and completing form

BR19.

It may be possible for you to pay Class 3 contributions for previous years to enable you to either qualify for a basic pension at the minimum rate or to increase the rate for which you have qualified. In this case, contact your local Social Security office.

Payment

There are two ways in which you can receive your pension:

- By direct payment into a bank, giro or building society cheque account. By this method you can choose to be paid every four or 13 weeks, however these payments are made in arrears.
- Weekly in cash at the post office in which case you will be issued with an order book. If for whatever reason an order is not cashed within three months, tell your local Social Security office without delay. If it is not cashed within 12 months you will lose the pension due unless you still have the order and can show a good cause for not having cashed it.

Going abroad

If you are going abroad for more than three months, advise your Social Security office in plenty of time so that they can make arrangements to get your pension paid to you abroad. Of course this does not apply if your pension is paid directly into an account.

If you are living abroad, you may only get any rate increases if:

- you are living in a European Community country including Gibraltar, or
- you are living in a country with which the UK has a

reciprocal agreement which allows you to receive the increased rate.

 INCREASING YOUR STATE PENSION

If you are in receipt of a company or private pension or other regular source of income, you may decide to give up your rights to the state pension in order to earn extra. The extra pension you earn is called **increments**. To get these increments you must:

- be either a woman under 65 or a man under 70
- usually live in Great Britain.

You can only apply to give up your pension once and will only earn increments after seven full weeks.

How much extra will I get?

For each year you give up your right to pension, the most extra you can earn is about 7.5p a week for every £1 of your pension. It is calculated by multiplying your weekly pension by 52 and dividing by 700. Thus a basic pension of £61.15 will earn an extra £4.54, entitling you to receive £65.69 when you resume receiving your pension.

Form N192 from the Social Security office will provide you with additional information and an application form.

 COMPANY AND PRIVATE PENSIONS
Company pensions

Company pension schemes may be either **contributory** or **non-contributory**, although these days more likely the latter. When you reach retirement or any previously agreed age, you will be entitled to receive the pension according to the rules and regulations of the scheme. Your company's personnel or human resources department will be able to give you all the necessary details.

You may have worked for several employers during your working life and have lost track of some of the pensions they have built up over the years. To trace a pension contact the Pension Schemes Registry on (0191) 225 6313 and they will send you a form *Tracing Your Old Pension*; fill it out and return it to them and there is every chance that they will be able to help you.

Private pensions

As with company pensions, the amount you receive will depend upon the scheme and how well your contributions have been invested by the pension company. You will probably be able to take your pension in part or in total as a **lump sum**. This is a decision you must make for yourself.

Taxation

It is important to remember that income you receive from company and private pensions and other sources, excluding any state pensions and benefits, may mean that you have to pay income tax if the total exceeds the allowances. For the tax year 2000–2001 the **Personal Age Allowance** for anyone between 65 and 74 is £5,790 and over 75 is £6,050. The income limit is £17,000.

 ADDITIONAL STATE BENEFITS

The whole area of state benefits is something of a minefield as they not only depend on your personal circumstances but each government makes regular changes to the rules and regulations. The following is only a guide and you would be advised to contact your local Social Security office to find out exactly what you are entitled to.

Graduated Retirement Benefit

This is based on the amount of NI contributions you made when the scheme existed between April 1961 and April 1975. If you were an employee and paid graduated NI contributions you will get a **Graduated Benefit Payment**. The amount you receive will depend on the number of contributions you paid between the above dates and the value of the unit at the time you claim your pension.

State Earnings-Related Pension Scheme (SERPS)

This is part of the pension which is earnings-related and as a member of SERPS you earn **Additional Pension**. You are entitled to this Additional Pension if you have paid standard rate Class 1 NI contributions in any tax year from 6 April 1978 to 5 April 1997 as an employee on earnings between the lower and upper earnings limits. If during this period you or your company contracted out of SERPS into an approved occupational or personal pension scheme, you will still be entitled to the Additional Pension. The calculations for working out this Additional Pension are complex and set out in booklet NP46.

Age Addition

Upon reaching the age of 80, your retirement pension will automatically be increased by an **Age Addition**.

Christmas Bonus

A tax-free bonus will be paid with your pension shortly before Christmas each year. Only one payment is made for each person. You may get an extra bonus if you are entitled to an increase for your spouse and you are both over state pension age by the end of the week in which the bonus is paid.

Income Support

If you and your spouse, if applicable, have an income which is below a certain level, you may be able to get **Income Support**. Whereas people under 60 must be available for work this restriction does not apply to people aged 60 or over. Also one should not have savings which currently exceed £12,000. The actual amount you receive would depend on a number of factors such as your age, whether you have a partner, any dependent children, your current income and any other benefits that you are receiving. People on Income Support may also be able to claim **Council Tax Benefit**, help with **mortgage interest payments** and **funeral expenses**. Leaflet IS20 *A Guide to Income Support* available from your local Social Security office will give you more details.

Winter Fuel Payment

This is a payment made to help with heating costs. Following a European ruling, both men and women will receive this payment automatically upon reaching the age of 60. It is normally paid each November/December and is currently £150 per household.

For other services contact your local council's Social Services department, your local advice centre or Age Concern for further information about:

- home care assistants
- meals-on-wheels
- aids to mobility
- social clubs and day centres

- special transport schemes
- residential homes.

 CONCESSIONS

In addition to pensions and state benefits, there are numerous other concessions available to help you save money. Some of these are applicable from the age of 60, others at the state pension age.

- Prescriptions – free from the age of 60.
- Eye tests – free from the age of 60.
- Rail travel – senior rail cards are available to those 60 or over, allowing you to travel at reduced rates on certain trains at certain times.
- Bus travel – many local transport services offer free or reduced cost travel to pensioners.
- Cinemas – most offer reduced ticket prices from the age of 60 for the afternoon performances.
- Places of interest – the majority of stately homes, castles, museums and other places of interest have concession entry fees.
- Garden centres and DIY stores – a number of these specify one day a week when senior citizens can make purchases at reduced rates.
- Hairdressers – many hairdressers set aside one morning a week and charge reduced rates for pensioners. If you are prepared to act as a model, you can get your hair cut and styled for free at many hair salons.
- Subscriptions – the National Trust, English Heritage and similar organisations have lower subscriptions for older people.

The above are just some of the concessions available, always ask if it is not made clear.

MAKING WHAT MATTERS WORK FOR YOU

✓ Make sure you receive all statement pension due to you.

✓ Consider ways you could increase your state pension.

✓ Check with your company about pension rights. Contact the Pension Scheme Registry for other company pensions which may be due to you. Decide the best way for you to take your company and/or private pension.

✓ Claim all state benefits to which you are entitled.

✓ Make full use of other concessions available to you.

3 Planning Your Finances

It is never too late to plan. The main thing is to make sure that you live comfortably within your means.

4

things that
really matter

1 **PLANNING YOUR INCOME AND OUTGOINGS**

2 **INVESTING FOR THE FUTURE**

3 **REDUCING THE TAX BURDEN**

4 **TAKING FINANCIAL ADVICE**

One of the major concerns that people have when they retire is **how they are going to live on their income**. For most people this income will be their pension. Whilst some people make plans for their financial future well before they retire, others do not.

Upon retirement your only source of income may be your pension, in which case you will need to carefully balance this with expenditures, reducing these if necessary to ensure that you are able to meet them. Remember if your income is low, you may be entitled to additional benefits as discussed in the previous chapter.

On the other hand, when you retire you may find yourself with a large amount of cash, having taken all or part of a company or private pension as a lump sum. You could of course put this money straight into the bank. However, it will be more beneficial to you if you **make it work for you** to earn more through investments of various types.

IS THIS YOU?

 • I can't live on my pension. • I'm going to have to reduce my standard of living. • I don't want to risk losing my money through bad investments. • How do I know what the future holds? • I want to leave something for my children. • I don't understand high finance and investments. • I am worried about being conned by unscrupulous advisers.

PLANNING YOUR INCOME AND OUTGOINGS

When you retire you will have a set, regular income such as your pensions. You will also have regular outgoings or expenditures, for example gas, electricity, rent, council tax, telephone and so on. Where some expenses differ slightly from month to month, use an average figure. With this information you can **work out your budget**, normally on a monthly basis. This will show you how much you have left over after paying your known outgoings.

Using simplified figures, a typical monthly budget may look something like this:

Income	£	£
Pensions	1,000	
Part-time work	500	1,500
Outgoings		
Rent	300	
Electricity	50	
Gas	30	
Council tax	50	
Telephone	20	
Housekeeping	250	700
Balance or residue		800

This shows that there is £800 each month for other

expenses such as entertainment, clothes, repairs, holidays and so on.

You may wish to take this a stage further and produce what is known in accounting terms as a **cash flow forecast**. This is really a series of monthly budgets but can include other less regular expenses. Again using simple figures, a cash flow forecast might look like this:

	May	June	July	Aug	Sept	Oct
Balance b/f	0	800	1,600	1,650	2,450	1,750
Income						
Pensions	1,000	1,000	1,000	1,000	1,000	1,000
P/t work	500	500	500	500	500	500
Total	1,500	2,300	3,100	3,150	3,950	3,250
Outgoings						
Rent	300	300	300	300	300	300
Electricity	50	50	50	50	50	50
Gas	30	30	30	30	30	30
Council tax	50	50	50	50	50	50
Telephone	20	20	20	20	20	20
Housekeeping	250	250	250	250	250	250
Repairs			750			
Holiday					1,500	
Total	700	700	1,450	700	2,200	700
Balance c/f	800	1,600	1,650	2,450	1,750	1,550

This shows the planned income and outgoings for the next six months. Simply add the balance or residue for each month to the income for the next. To keep a check, compare your actual income and outgoings with the plan and adjust future plans accordingly.

Budgets and cash flow forecasts will enable you to plan for the future and ensure that you have funds to meet unexpected expenses.

 INVESTING FOR THE FUTURE

Before making any investments, you must decide what your requirements are. You may need a regular income, one or more lump sums at future dates or a combination of these. You also need to decide how much you can afford to invest and whether this will be made as a lump sum at the beginning or a series of smaller amounts at regular intervals. This will determine the type of investments which will suit you best.

Banks, building societies and other financial institutions offer a wide range of products designed to meet all needs. These range from simple schemes where you can invest and withdraw your cash at will, but earning only a low rate of interest, to investments in stocks, bonds, etc offering a much higher rate but with restricted withdrawal facilities or maturing at set dates in the future. It is worth remembering that the higher the interest or return, the higher the risk. You could earn a great deal of money by investing in stocks and shares but you could also lose everything, as investors in Lloyds found to their cost several years ago.

You must decide how much of a gamble you are prepared to take.

If you are not sure what to do, take professional advice. **Individual Savings Accounts**, or **ISAs**, are a way to save and invest tax-free. The scheme was introduced by the government in April 1999 and replaces TESSAs and PEPs and is guaranteed for at least ten years. There are two main types of ISA, the **Mini** and the **Maxi**.

- **Mini ISAs**. There are three separate Mini ISAs:
  - cash: which builds up interest similar to a savings account
  - life insurance: money invested on life insurance policies
  - stocks and shares: money invested on the stock market.
- **Maxi ISAs**. These are a combination of the above.

Depending on the type you choose there are limits to the amount you can invest.

ISAs are available from banks, building societies, other financial institutions and even some supermarket chains. Read their literature carefully to make sure that they meet the **CAT standards**. These are voluntary standards introduced by the government to ensure that the providers are giving you fair **charges**, easy **access** and decent **terms**. The literature will also give details of maximum and minimum amounts that can be invested.

ISAs were introduced to encourage everyone to save for the future. The main benefit is that, unlike other investments, the interest earned is free of all tax.

 REDUCING THE TAX BURDEN

Unfortunately, retirement does not necessarily mean that you will escape the clutches of the Inland Revenue. You may still be liable to pay tax on your income. However, your Personal Allowance, also known as Age Allowance, increases from the age of 65 and again from 75.

- **Non-taxable income**. The state retirement pension is not liable for income tax. As we have already seen, interest received from ISA investments is also exempt from tax.
- **Taxable income**. All other income received from private or company pensions, share dividends, earned income, etc is liable for income tax if the total exceeds the Age Allowance.
- **Capital Gains Tax**. Profit made from selling assets such as shares and property, with the exception of your home, may be liable for Capital Gains Tax. However, there is an **Annual Exemption**. If the total profits for the year do not exceed a figure set by the government, currently £7,100 per person, no tax is payable. Therefore to avoid having to pay this tax, plan your sales so that the Annual Exemption is not exceeded. Alternatively, hold some of your assets in your spouse's name, then each of you could sell them and thereby double the profit before reaching the exemption figure. The tax payable on the excess profit depends upon the number of years for which the assets have been held. Assets held for two years or less are liable to 100% tax, assets held for ten or more years are liable to 60%. This is known as Tapering Relief.
- **Inheritance Tax**. This is covered in detail in Chapter 6.

If you are unsure of your tax situation, seek help from a qualified accountant or your local Inland Revenue office.

 TAKING FINANCIAL ADVICE

If you have a sum of money that you wish to invest you would do well to take professional advice from an expert. There are basically two types of financial advisers.

- **In-Company**. These people are employed by a bank or other financial institution and, whilst giving you sound advice, will only be promoting their company's products.
- **Independent**. Not being tied to a particular bank or building society, they will be able to offer a wider range of investment products to suit your requirements.

Before seeking advice:

- Choose your adviser carefully, preferably on recommendation.
- Determine your needs, eg a regular monthly or annual income.
- Decide how much you wish to invest and what risk you can afford to take.

It is sensible to take advice from more than one consultant to enable you to compare their recommendations and decide exactly what is right for you.

MAKING WHAT MATTERS WORK FOR YOU

✓ Plan your income and expenditure for each week or month. Keep careful records of what comes in and what goes out.

✓ Consider what investments you might make.

✓ Remember to allow for any tax due and get help and advice if necessary.

✓ Obtain expert advice before making any investments.

4 Relocating

*It is the dream of many people to move home
once they have retired.*

Is it the cottage with roses round the door, a bungalow by the sea or a warden controlled retirement village? Whatever the reason, moving home is a stressful business and the older we get, the more stressful it can become. Unfortunately the expectations and the reality are not always the same. There are many things to be considered before taking the plunge to ensure that the dream does not become a nightmare.

Before relocating, think very carefully about **what you want to achieve by moving** and if it will be worth all the upheaval. If you do decide to move, take your time, there is no rush. Spend some time in the area that you hope to move to and discover for yourself whether or not it offers all you want and need. Remember that moving costs money, so you cannot afford to make mistakes.

IS THIS YOU?

• I need to move to a smaller house. • I would like to live by the sea. • My ideal home is a cottage in the country. • I would feel safer if I moved to another area. • I want to be nearer to my family. • I would prefer to live in a warmer climate.

① DECIDING THE REASONS FOR MOVING HOME

There can be a number of reasons why you might wish to relocate when you retire, such as to:

- be nearer your family, especially grandchildren
- move away from your family
- have a smaller property with less upkeep
- be in a quieter area in the countryside
- be with more people of your own age group
- feel safer and more secure
- be in a less expensive part of the country
- live in a more conducive climate
- simply leave the area in which you currently live.

Whatever the reason, make sure it is the right one.

Let's now look at some of the benefits of relocating:

- If you propose to move to a smaller property or to an area where property prices are cheaper, this will free up some of your capital which can be invested for your future.
- A move to a smaller property should mean less costs in heating, lighting and general maintenance.
- By moving to a quieter area you can escape many of the pressures of urban living, such as traffic and noise.
- Warden controlled properties will give you a greater sense of security.

- You will be able to see more of your family the closer you live to them.
- If you suffer from arthritis or similar aches and pains, a move to a warmer climate can be very beneficial.
- There may be more suitable social activities in the new location.
- Moving to a different area could give you a new lease of life.

 WHAT NEEDS TO BE DONE

It may be some years since you last moved home, so here is a reminder of what you need to do.

Invite two or three local estate agents to value your property. Place your property with the most suitable estate agent – the one who has a good local reputation, is used to handling your type of property, gives you a sensible valuation and charges competitive rates. Advise your solicitor of your intentions and check their costs for conveyancing.

Make sure your property, including the garden, is clean, tidy and welcoming for prospective buyers. You should not need to redecorate, but a touch of paint here and there might help. List any fixtures and fittings, including garden plants and shrubs, that you intend taking with you. This should be made available to all prospective purchasers.

Make a list of what you want from your new home. Visit estate agents in the area you intend moving to and arrange to view as many suitable properties as possible. Always make an offer below the asking price, you may be lucky.

Once you have decided on one or two properties, check with the owners what they intend to take with them so that there are no nasty surprises when you move in.

Having exchanged contracts on your property and the one you are buying, obtain quotations from a number of reputable removal companies. Again check what they will do for the quoted price and that they have insurance for any damaged articles.

This is now the time to get rid of all your unwanted junk, so have a good sort out. Notify all friends, relatives, banks, building societies and other relevant organisations and institutions of your new address. Cancel the newspapers, milk and any other home deliveries. Advise the gas, electricity and telephone companies of your move, and arrange for all these services to be functioning when you move in to your new home. Arrange with the Royal Mail to have your mail redirected to your new address.

All that remains is to pay the bills and move.

 THINGS TO LOOK OUT FOR

When contemplating relocation, there are a number of things to be considered, not least of which is the cost. Costs of moving include:

- fee to estate agent for selling your property
- solicitor's fee for conveyancing
- Stamp Duty which is a percentage of the value of the property you are purchasing
- removal costs.

When moving to another part of the country, you need to take into account other things such as:

- You will have to change your doctor, dentist, optician.
- The time may come when you cannot or will not wish to drive your car, so what public transport is available?
- The proximity of shops, library and other services.

- You could be leaving long-time friends behind.
- You will need to familiarise yourself with your new environment, join clubs and make new friends.
- You will probably have to spend money making your new home as you want it to be.

④ MOVING ABROAD

The thought of living in a country where the weather is warm and the cost of living lower than the UK can be very tempting.

For some people this is the right choice to make. However, there is a great difference between spending a holiday in another country and actually living there. Before deciding to relocate to Spain, Portugal, the Canaries or somewhere similar, go and stay there for at least three months, preferably on a self-catering basis. Many tour companies offer such opportunities to the over-60s.

Whilst you are there, get first-hand information about:
- that country's property laws
- local and regional taxation
- costs of gas, electricity and other services
- details of medical and dental services – do the local doctors speak English?
- availability and costs of different foodstuffs and household items.

These countries usually have a number of ex-patriot communities, so get to know the people, discover what social activities are available and then ask yourself if these will be sufficient to satisfy your needs.

You must also **ask yourself what you will miss about leaving Britain**. Once you have committed yourself, sold your home in the UK and moved to another country, it can be very difficult to return.

There are of course benefits to relocating to another country in southern Europe, not least being a milder climate. This means that you can spend more time out of doors and less money on heating and warm clothes. A further benefit is that most items are cheaper than in Britain.

- Should you decide to live abroad you will need to make the necessary arrangements regarding your state pension and banking.
- Ideally, if your finances will allow, rent out your property in the UK or buy a small flat. This will enable you to return after a year or two if things do not work out as you had hoped.
- Some people buy a recreational vehicle and spend half the year on the Continent, staying for a month or two in each place, and return to their home in the UK for the rest of the year and so have the best of both worlds.

You may decide to move much further afield to Australia, New Zealand or Canada. The reason for this is normally to be closer to your children and their families. You will need to contact the appropriate High Commissions in London to find out what will be involved in such a move.

MAKING WHAT MATTERS WORK FOR YOU

✓ Make sure that your reasons for moving are the right ones.

✓ Spend time in different areas before deciding to move. Calculate the costs of relocating before doing so.

✓ When deciding on a place to live, remember to look to the future when you may not be as fit and mobile as you are now. If you do intend to relocate, do so as soon as practical whilst you are still young enough to accept the upheaval and adapt to your new home.

✓ Think very carefully before deciding to live abroad.

5 Protecting Yourself and Your Property

Now is the time to check that you have made
everything as safe as you can.

6

things that
really matter

1 **PROTECTING YOUR HOME**

2 **SECURING YOUR PERSONAL PROPERTY**

3 **PROTECTING YOUR CAR AND OTHER VEHICLES**

4 **LEAVING YOUR HOME UNOCCUPIED**

5 **AVOIDING BOGUS CALLERS**

6 **TAKING PERSONAL PRECAUTIONS**

It is always important to make sure that your home and property are as secure as possible from crime. However, the older we get the more vulnerable we feel and become to criminals.

The risk of becoming a victim of crime is low in the UK compared to many other countries. Similarly crime is more rife in large towns and cities than elsewhere. Nevertheless you need to take every possible precaution to reduce the risk. Statistics show that 80% of crimes against property and vehicles are carried out by opportunist thieves, that is those who see an open window or other easy access. Although very traumatic when they occur, crimes against the person are fortunately rare. Again **there are measures that you can take to reduce that risk**.

Protecting your property does cost money, however most insurance companies offer premium reductions on homes that are well secured.

IS THIS YOU?

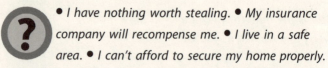

- *I have nothing worth stealing.* • *My insurance company will recompense me.* • *I live in a safe area.* • *I can't afford to secure my home properly.*
- *It's the job of the police to protect me and my property.*

PROTECTING YOUR HOME

When a Crime Prevention Officer visits a property, he or she will take an 'onion peel' approach. First they will look at the boundaries and garden, then the exterior of the house and finally the interior. So we will take the same approach.

Boundaries

Ensure that all walls, fences and gates surrounding your garden are in good condition and preferably at least two metres in height. Defensive planting along the boundaries provides an excellent deterrent. Prickly shrubs such as berberis, Spanish gorse, firethorn pyracantha, white bramble and climbing and rambling roses are all ideal. They should be allowed to grow to about 1 metre in width to prevent people from climbing over them. This is especially important if your garden backs on to an open space or public byway. Avoid tall hedges along the front boundary as this could provide cover for anyone trying to break in at the front of your house.

Gardens

Never leave a garage or garden shed unlocked as they often contain expensive tools ideal for breaking in to the rest of the house. Fit all shed and garage doors with a strong padlock and make sure they are solid enough not to be kicked in. Always lock ladders inside your garage or shed to prevent them being used by the thief.

Windows

A third of burglars gain access through a back window. Fit key-operated locks to all downstairs windows and those upstairs above a flat roof or by a drainpipe. Louvre windows are especially vulnerable as the slats can be easily removed. Glue the slats in place with an epoxy resin and fit a special louvre lock. As a final resort you may consider fitting a decorative, wrought iron grill to vulnerable windows.

Doors

Fit the back and front doors with five-lever mortice deadlocks and use them. Bolts should also be fitted top and bottom to all exterior doors. You will need to get specialist advice on fitting locks to patio doors. If you have glass on or around any exterior doors, make sure the glass is laminated. Fit a security chain to the front door. Check the door hinges to make sure they are strong and well secured. Letter box cages prevent thieves from putting their hands through the letter box and trying to open the locks from inside.

Burglar alarms

Visible burglar alarms are a good deterrent as they will make the potential house-breaker think twice. There are many systems available, from cheap DIY ones to more sophisticated and expensive ones. Wired alarms are cheaper, but easily installed 'wire free' systems are readily available, whereby sensors are fitted around the house and transmit radio detection signals to a control system. Before having an alarm installed, get specialist advice and several quotes.

A badly fitted alarm can create problems in itself. Unless you have the necessary skills and knowledge, do not attempt to install a DIY system yourself. If you truly cannot afford a full alarm system, a dummy box fitted to the front of the house is better than nothing as a deterrent in itself.

Security lighting

The simplest and cheapest lighting is a light over the front door or porch. However, for greater security consider fitting one or more exterior lights with infra-red sensors that switch the lights on when they detect anything within their range. Many such systems can be adjusted to prevent them coming on when a cat or bat crosses their beam.

Indoors

Most burglaries happen when a property is empty. Use time switches to turn on lights, radios and other appliances when you are out. Keep valuable items out of sight from anyone looking in the window. Never leave spare keys where they can be easily seen from outside.

Flats

If you live in a flat the most vulnerable part is the front door, so ensure that it is strong with good locks and bolts. You could consider strengthening the door with a steel strip. If possible install a door telephone entry system.

 SECURING YOUR PERSONAL PROPERTY

Most burglars will be in and out of a house within three minutes.

The opportunist thief will take those items that they can most easily sell. These tend to be TVs, videos, hi-fi systems and cameras. The professional will tend to go for jewellery and valuable ornaments. Although there is little you can do once the thief has broken in, don't make it easy for them. Never leave cash, cheque books, credit cards or keys lying about the house. Don't keep your most valuable pieces of jewellery in the obvious box on the dressing table. Hide them in the loft, for example, or even under the dirty washing in the laundry basket.

Although the chances of the thief being caught are small, the police do recover large quantities of stolen goods but have great difficulty in tracing the owners. To give yourself a better chance of recovering stolen property, **mark them with your post code**. There are several methods of marking items including engraving or etching, ultra violet marking and special pens for marking glass, china and other glazed surfaces. Property marking kits are available from most DIY stores.

In addition to marking valuable items such as jewellery, clocks and watches, silver and gold ware, ceramics and antique furniture, **take colour photographs** of each item and keep them in a safe place. If you own any paintings record the exact size, details of the subject, the medium (oils, watercolours, acrylic), the artist's name and a description of the frame.

 PROTECTING YOUR CAR AND OTHER VEHICLES
Cars
Car theft is one of the highest reported crimes in the United Kingdom. one car is stolen every minute (I don't know who owns it but they really must be more careful). There are basically four categories of car crime:

- Joyriders – young people, mainly boys, who steal and

drive away cars simply for the thrill. These cars are usually recovered but are often badly damaged.

- Car theft – these are usually stolen by opportunist thieves who hope to sell the car either as a whole or in parts. Professionals will steal a car as a 'getaway' vehicle for another crime.
- Theft from cars – again usually opportunists who see something of value lying in the car. Forty per cent of car break-ins involve the theft of mobile phones.
- Theft to order – these are professionals who steal specific cars, usually expensive, luxury vehicles and have a ready buyer, often overseas.

There are many ways in which you can reduce the likelihood of your car being stolen or broken into.

- Always remove the ignition key, even when parked in your garage or paying for petrol.
- If you have a garage, use it for its intended purpose, very few cars are stolen from locked garages.
- Never leave valuable items, briefcases, handbags, coats etc on view in your car, lock them in the boot.
- If your car is not fitted with an immobiliser, get one fitted and switch it on each time you park your car.
- Fit and use steering wheel and/or gear locks, they act as deterrents.
- Have the vehicle identification number or registration number visibly etched on all windows, this will act as a deterrent as the thief will have to replace them.
- If possible, remove the radio/cassette/CD player when you park and leave it in the boot. These are among the most regular items stolen from cars.
- When parking, even at home, turn on the car alarm if one is fitted, although their value is open to debate as

many people ignore the sound.

- Fit lockable wheel-nuts especially if you have expensive, alloy wheels.
- Tracking devices enable the police to trace stolen vehicles.
- Avoid parking in dark, unlit areas wherever possible.

Bicycles

When at home, keep your bicycles in a locked garage or shed. If you have neither of these, store them in your hallway. Wherever you are, always lock your unattended bicycle with a strong chain and padlock. Lock it to railings or a lamp-post if possible.

Caravans

To make sure that your caravan cannot be towed away:

- Lock the coupling head into a cover.
- Use lock nuts and a clamp on the wheels.
- You could also have a tracking device fitted.
- Etch all windows with a security number.

To prevent thieves from breaking in:

- Always close all windows, doors and roof lights.
- Fit secure locks to the door and windows.
- Keep all valuables and documents out of sight.

 **LEAVING YOUR HOME UNOCCUPIED**

The majority of house break-ins occur when the owners are out.

Don't advertise the fact that you are away on holiday or even out at work or shopping. The burglar will look for tell-tale signs which show a house or flat is empty.

There are several **steps you can take** if you are going to be away for a few days or more:

- Shut and lock all doors and windows.
- Use time switches to turn on lights and other appliances.
- Keep your TV, video etc out of sight.
- Hide jewellery and other valuables in unlikely places, or leave them with a trusted friend.
- Cancel all deliveries of newspapers, milk etc.

Ask a friend or neighbour to make sure that all mail and newspapers are pushed through the letter box. If you have a glass front door, get them to collect your mail as a pile of letters and other post lying on the mat can easily be seen through the door and is a sure sign of your absence. Ask them to keep a general eye on your home whilst you are away and if possible give them a contact phone number. Do not close the curtains as this would not be normal during daylight hours and gives another signal to the burglar.

If you are out for a short time, shopping, visiting friends, working and so on:

- Shut and lock all doors and windows.
- Use time switches if appropriate.
- Avoid notes in milk bottles and similar signs.
- Never leave keys under mats, hanging on string inside the letter box or anywhere else where they could be found by potential thieves.
- Draw the curtains if you are going out for the evening.

On returning home to an empty house:

- Press the door bell or knock on the door. If there is an intruder inside, they will leave quickly to avoid confrontation.
- If there are signs of intrusion when you return, do not

enter the house but go to a neighbour or public phone box and contact the police.
– When arriving home by taxi or if a friend drops you off, ask them to wait until you are inside the house.

 AVOIDING BOGUS CALLERS

Unlike most house breakers, the bogus caller is a professional criminal and has planned his or her intended crime. Such people tend to prey on the elderly as they are generally more vulnerable and trusting.

Fortunately, the majority of callers are genuine but they could be confidence tricksters or thieves, so beware as their purpose is to con you out of money or steal from your home.

Before answering the door, **look through a window or spy hole** if you have one. If you do not recognise the caller, put the security chain on before opening the door.

There are several types of bogus callers:

Bogus 'officials'

These people may or may not wear a uniform and claim to be from the gas, water or electricity board, the council, health authority or a similar organisation. **Always ask to see their identity card**. If they don't have one they will leave very smartly. Take any proffered card and examine it closely. If you are still uncertain, tell them that you will check with their company. Genuine callers will happily accept this. Look up the number in your telephone directory, the one on the card may be that of an accomplice. Only when you are sure of their identity, let them into your home.

Bogus 'workmen'

Their usual story is that they are working nearby and have noticed that your roof, chimney, gutters or windows need urgent repairs. They will offer to do the job immediately, and quote an inflated price for the work and ask for all or part of the money in advance. If you tell them that you do not have the money with you, they may offer to drive you to your bank or building society to withdraw it for them. They will either disappear or carry out a very cheap and shoddy repair. The best way to deal with these people is to politely thank them for the information, **ask them for their card and a written quotation** saying that you will obtain other quotes and get back to them. Your chances of seeing them again are zero.

Bogus 'dealers'

Often posing as antique dealers they will offer to buy your antiques, furniture or jewellery and will offer you what may seem a good price but will be a lot less than its real value. Never let them into your home, simply **say that you do not wish to sell anything**. If you do want to sell something, ask one or two genuine dealers to value it properly.

Bogus 'sellers'

Before arranging to see anyone selling insurance, home improvements or similar, check very carefully with their company first. They may seem very plausible as they sit talking to you but they could have an ulterior motive. If they ask to use your toilet which is upstairs, discretely accompany them to make sure that they do not go into any other rooms. They may not take anything there and then but could be casing the place for a future break-in.

Other callers

If a stranger comes to your door asking for a glass of water or to use your toilet, you would be well advised to politely decline.

Sometimes bogus callers work in pairs. One acts as the 'distracter' keeping your attention whilst their colleague steals your property. Never let yourself be pressured by anyone who appears to be in a hurry. **If you have any suspicions at all, don't let them in**. When they have gone call a neighbour or friend to warn them. Do not hesitate to call the police if you believe that the caller had criminal intentions.

It is very unfortunate that we have to treat everyone with suspicion but **to be safe, be sure**.

 TAKING PERSONAL PRECAUTIONS

As has already been said, crimes against the person are fortunately comparatively rare. However there are **precautions that you can take** to reduce even this small risk.

Walking:

- Walk confidently, a positive manner could deter a potential attacker.
- Keep to well lit, populated places and avoid short cuts through dark, deserted areas as much as possible.
- If you hear footsteps behind you, turn round and face the person, again this could deter any likely attacker.
- Always walk facing the traffic. If a driver stops to talk to you, stay at least an arm's length from the vehicle.
- If you carry a personal attack alarm, always have it readily available.
- If you think you are being followed, cross the road or

change direction and make for a busy place.

- Should someone snatch your handbag or other property, give it up rather than risk injury.

Using public transport:

- Keep tight hold of any bags or cases you are carrying.
- On buses try to sit near the driver or at least on the lower deck.
- On trains avoid empty compartments or those containing only one or two suspicious looking individuals.
- When waiting on platforms or at bus stops try to keep in well lit areas or near groups of people.
- If there is an incident, inform the driver or another person immediately.

Using taxis:

- Use 'black cabs' wherever possible.
- When booking a mini-cab, always ask the company for the driver's name, call sign and make of car.
- Never accept a lift from a mini-cab touting for business, this is not only illegal but could put you in danger.

Driving alone:

- Check that all doors and windows are locked, especially at night.
- Keep your vehicle regularly serviced to reduce breakdowns.
- Never pick up hitch hikers however genuine they may look.
- Have a car phone or mobile phone to summon help in emergencies.
- If you believe you are being followed, drive to the nearest town and look for the police station.
- Beware of anyone who tries to flag you down, is the

accident genuine? It may be safer to stay in your car and
phone for help.

- If you break down on a motorway and do not have your
own phone, walk to the nearest emergency phone to get
help, remembering to lock the car before you leave it.

Men can help by taking care not to unintentionally frighten
women and can take steps to make them feel safer:

- When walking in the same direction as a woman, do not
walk behind her. Cross the road and walk on the other
side.
- Do not sit next to a lone woman on a bus or train if
possible.
- Be wary about talking to a woman, even if it is just to
ask a question or for directions. She will not know your
intentions.
- If you wish to offer assistance to a woman in a broken
down car, keep your distance from her. Preferably offer
to phone for help.
- Help female friends and relatives by giving them lifts or
walking with them.

MAKING WHAT MATTERS WORK FOR YOU

✓ Secure your home by fitting good locks to all doors and windows. Spend as much as you can afford on security.

✓ Check your insurance policies to make sure that everything is properly covered. Read the small print carefully. Mark and keep a record of all property including TVs, cameras, jewellery and all other valuables. Never leave cash, purses, wallets or keys lying about the house.

✓ Protect your car by fitting immobilisers and other security devices. Keep all valuables out of sight in the boot. Lock your car every time you leave it.

✓ Avoid leaving tell-tale signs that your home is unoccupied.

✓ Don't be taken in by bogus callers. Always check their credentials.

✓ Avoid putting yourself in vulnerable situations when you are outdoors. Security is a matter of being sensible.

6 Settling Your Affairs

It is a common sense step to ensure an orderly arrangement of your affairs.

5 things that really matter

1 THE IMPORTANCE OF MAKING A WILL

2 REDUCING THE TAX BURDEN

3 WRITING A SIMPLE WILL

4 CHANGING YOUR WILL

5 KEEPING YOUR AFFAIRS IN ORDER

Many people believe that making a will is equivalent to signing their own death warrant. It is not.

A will is a legal document which sets out in detail to whom you wish to leave your estate upon your death. Your estate consists of your cash, including all bank and savings accounts, together with all of your assets such as houses, cars, shares, furniture, jewellery and all other personal effects.

Anyone over the age of 18 and 'being of sound mind' can make a will. Being of sound mind is defined as being fully aware of what one is doing.

A will can be simple, such as leaving everything to your next of kin, or detailed to the point of nominating specific books to be left to named people. You can of course leave your estate to whom you wish, however it is wise to take advice in certain circumstances as wills can be contested.

It is vitally important to make a will as this reduces the problems and difficulties to those you leave behind upon your demise.

IS THIS YOU?

*● I have nothing worth leaving. ● How do I go
about making a will? ● Where can I get help?
● I really must get down to it. ● It's too expensive
and complicated. ● I'm leaving everything to my wife so I
don't need a will.*

THE IMPORTANCE OF MAKING A WILL

A will is a legal document, detailing how you wish your
estate to be settled upon your death. The making of a will is
a comparatively simple process, yet almost two-thirds of
people in the UK die without one. There could be several
reasons for this.

Many people believe that their estate will automatically
go to their spouse when they die. Others genuinely have
nothing to leave. Some have no close relatives or friends
and could not care less what happens when they die. A
number think that only rich people leave wills. However, the
main reason is that the person has 'just not got round to
making one'.

You do not have to wait until you are getting old before
making a will, you can always alter it later if you wish.

Some **good reasons for making a will** include to:

- make life simpler for your family on your death
- ensure your property goes to the people you want to
  benefit
- ensure your spouse is not deprived of his/her home
- ensure a common law partner benefits as you would
  wish
- ensure specific gifts pass to whom you wish
- ensure funeral expenses are paid from your estate
- ensure that your property does not go to unknown
  relatives

- minimise tax on your estate
- ensure your assets are properly managed
- give you peace of mind
- help your affairs to be settled quickly
- ensure any change in circumstances do not accidentally revoke your wishes.

Any person who dies without making a will is said to have died **intestate**. In such cases, the estate is subject to the laws of intestacy. These laws or rules were drawn up in 1925 and are therefore outdated as they do not take into consideration the changes that have taken place in family relationships in recent years. However, they still apply and the only things that have altered are the sums of money involved.

Under these laws, when a person dies without making a will, leaving a spouse and children, the surviving spouse will receive the personal chattels and the first £125,000 plus a life interest in half the estate with the remainder being shared between the children. If there are no children, the spouse receives the first £200,000 with the remainder being distributed among the nearest relatives. Chattels are things such as furniture, the car and other personal effects. If the family home is owned as a **joint tenancy** or **tenancy in common**, the laws as described in section 2 below apply.

The laws of intestacy include a set order in which relatives can benefit from the estate. This is:

- spouse
- children (including illegitimate and adopted)
- parents
- brothers and sisters
- half-brothers and sisters
- grandparents

- uncles and aunts (full-blood)
- uncles and aunts (half-blood).

If any of the above die before you, then their children, if any, will benefit. Where there is no surviving spouse or children, efforts must be made to find relatives who could benefit from the estate. It could happen that the eventual beneficiary is a distant cousin, nephew or niece that the deceased person may not have seen for many years or even knew existed.

To benefit as a spouse under the intestacy laws, he or she must have been legally married to the deceased. The law does not take into account common law partners.

Problems caused by intestacy include:

- If there is no will, members of the family will have to sort out the estate.
- Unless the right provisions have been made, the home may have to be sold to meet taxation and other costs.
- All bank and building society accounts will be frozen (unless they are joint accounts) until probate is granted.
- The spouse may be left with insufficient funds with which to live and maintain the home.
- it will take more time to administer the estate than if there had been a will.
- It may be necessary to engage the services of solicitors to locate distant relatives. This will cost money.

All in all, as I am sure you will agree, **it is well worth spending a little time and effort to make a will**.

 REDUCING THE TAX BURDEN

The estate of every deceased person, whether they die having made a will or intestate, is subject to **Inheritance**

Tax. This has replaced death or estate duties and the Capital Transfer Tax.

Two bands of taxation are applied to the value of the estate and these are set by the government. The bands for tax year 2000–2001 are:

- The first £234,000: nil-rated
- The residue: 40%

Thus if a man leaves an estate valued at £500,000, the tax payable will be 40% of £266,000, i.e. £106,400.

There are, however, legal and acceptable ways of reducing the total amount upon which tax is payable.

Property

Probably one's most valuable asset is the family home, be it a house, bungalow or flat. If when a person dies they are the **sole owner** of such property, the value of that property will be added to the total value of the estate for taxation. This could mean selling the home in order to meet the tax. However, if the property is held in **joint tenancy**, usually with one's spouse, the surviving spouse becomes the sole owner and it does not form part of the estate. Alternatively, the property could be held in **tenancy in common** with two or more named people. This means that each person owns an agreed percentage of the property. Thus when one of them dies, only the percentage that they own is valued for tax purposes. For example, if two people own a house as tenants in common with each having a 50% share and it is valued at £200,000, when one of them dies only their share of £100,000 becomes part of the estate. It is well worth making arrangements if you have not already done so.

Joint accounts

As with the joint tenancies, any bank or building society accounts held jointly become the property of the surviving account holders and so the amounts do not form part of the deceased person's estate.

Gifts

A popular method of reducing one's estate is by making gifts during one's lifetime. All gifts made seven years before death are exempt from tax. Unfortunately, we are not given a seven-year-warning of our impending demise. Gifts made less than seven years before death are taxed at 20% according to a sliding scale of years as follows:

Years	0–3	3–4	4–5	5–6	6–7
% of charge	100	80	60	40	20

If a gift of £5,000 was made in the fifth year before death, the tax would be 20% of £2,000 (which is 40% of £5,000) viz £400.

Exemptions

There are however a number of exemptions which apply and no tax is payable. These include:

- Unlimited amounts to your spouse.
- A total of £3,000 in any one tax year to any number of people.
- Small gifts up to £250 per person in any one tax year.
- Wedding gifts: maximum of £5,000 per child
                    maximum £2,500 per grandchild
                    maximum of £1,000 to other persons.
- Unlimited sums to registered charities.
- Unlimited sums to national heritage organisations.
- Unlimited sums to political parties although this is

limited to £100,000 in the year before death.

- Business/agricultural relief at 100% or 50% depending upon the circumstances. It is important to take professional advice in such cases.

Taxable gifts can be left 'free of tax' which means that the tax is paid from the estate or 'subject to tax' in which case the recipient is liable for the tax. If this tax is not paid within 12 months, the deceased person's 'personal representatives', usually the executors, become liable which can be very embarrassing for all concerned.

Care needs to be taken when making gifts, for if it is considered that the donor is continuing to benefit from the gift, its value may be added to the estate. For example, if a man gifts his house to another person but continues to live there until he dies, the value of the house will be included for tax purposes.

If you have a valuable estate and wish to reduce the tax burden, then perhaps making specific gifts could be one answer.

 WRITING A SIMPLE WILL

A **simple will** is one that is confined to leaving specific assets to named beneficiaries without any conditions or frills.

Who?

To make a will you must have something to leave and be the sole owner of those assets. Once these conditions have been fulfilled, a will can be made by:

- Any sane person over the age of 18 including prisoners and UK citizens living abroad.
- Armed Forces personnel under the age of 18 if on active

service.

- Foreigners with land or property in the UK who wish it to be disposed of according to English law.

What?

You can dispose of all of your assets in your will.

- **Money**: you can leave specific sums to named people.
- **Buildings**: providing you are the sole owner of any houses, flats or other buildings, you can leave them to whom you wish.
- **Land**: as with buildings.
- **Insurance policies**: unless the policy states that only certain people, such as your spouse, can benefit from any money payable on your death, you can bequeath any money due on your death.
- **Shares**: normally these can be bequeathed as you wish; there may be certain restrictions on how they can be disposed of, especially shares held in a private company.
- **Personal items**: antiques, jewellery, books, in fact any personal goods can be left to whom you wish. However, the law states that if there is insufficient money to cover any outstanding debts, personal items must be sold to recover the amounts due.
- **Instructions**: your will can contain instructions such as how you wish your body to be disposed of, funeral details and so on.

How?

There are several ways of making such a will.

You can **do-it-yourself**: will-making kits are sold by most major stationers and by following the instructions enclosed, should cause no problems. You can of course write your will on an ordinary piece of paper. It is important to get the wording right to avoid any misinterpretations or confusions in the future. Remember, **to be legally valid your will must be dated and signed by you in the presence of two witnesses simultaneously who must also sign your will**.

It is better to use the services of a **solicitor** for even the simplest of wills as they know how to construct them to prevent any future problems. Solicitors tend to use archaic terms and phrases, the reason being that such terms, through constant use over many years, are universally accepted and understood in law. Again in the interests of clarity, apart from beginning sentences with capital letters and ending them with full stops, solicitors do not use punctuation. Incorrect punctuation can lead to difficulties in interpretation of the testator's intent. Solicitors will normally charge between £40 and £60 for writing a simple will. They will also hold a copy on your behalf at no extra cost.

Will writing agencies provide a similar service to solicitors, usually coming to your home to prepare the will. Although they should be well versed in writing wills they do not necessarily have a legal qualification and will sometimes charge for holding a copy of the will.

Content

Apart from some standard legal phrases that it is customary to use, you are free to write your wish as you wish. The following list is a guide as to what should be included and in what order.

- Begin by stating that this is your last will and testament.
- Your full name and current address and the date on which the will is being made.

- A statement revoking all former wills made by you.
- The appointment of your executors, and trustees if relevant, together with any provision for payment.
- Instruction regarding your funeral or disposal of your body.
- You may wish to include a statement expressing your thanks to people not included in your bequests.
- Full details of the disposal of your estate.
- The 'Thirty Day Clause' (see below).
- Naming a beneficiary for any residue after all gifts have been allocated and expenses met.
- Finally your signature together with those of two witnesses.

The Thirty Day Clause: in the unlikely event that your main or sole beneficiary, such as your spouse, should die within 30 days of your death, the wishes expressed in his or her will will 'kick in' and the bequests made to your spouse could pass to people contrary to your wishes. Similarly, if your spouse had not made a will, then everything you left him/her will automatically go to his or her relations.

To prevent this happening, you can make a provision in your will appointing another beneficiary should your spouse not survive you by 30 days.

④ **CHANGING YOUR WILL**

Many people believe that once having made their will they can put it away and forget about it. However, it is advisable to check it every two or three years as your circumstances and wishes may have changed.

There are many reasons why your circumstances could change:

Divorce invalidates any benefits to a former spouse

within the existing will unless you have made special provisions. You may decide that you would still like to leave something to him or her when you die, so you must make a new will to include such provisions. Otherwise any bequests to your ex-spouse will go directly to your children (if any).

When you get **married**, any will that you have previously made becomes invalid and you need to write a new one. Although there are exceptions, it is easier to make a new will.

Death: should an original beneficiary die before you, unless you have made provision for this in your will it will be necessary to appoint another beneficiary to inherit that gift.

If you have **additional children or grandchildren** since making your will, you may need to include them in a new will.

Change of assets: since making your will you may have acquired new or disposed of original assets, so a new will should be made to reflect this.

Change of mind: you may decide, for whatever reason, to disinherit an original beneficiary and leave that bequest to someone else.

If you wish to change your will, you can either make an entirely new one or write a **codicil**. This is an addition or supplement to the original will. It must be prepared on a separate sheet of paper and signed and witnessed in the same way as your will. Although a correctly drafted codicil has the same validity as the will, there can be complications. It is always advisable therefore to make a new will. When you do so, make sure that you destroy the original will together with all copies. The law states that when destroying a will, preferably by burning it, it must be intentional, that is, not accidental. Should the original will be accidentally lost or destroyed, a copy is normally accepted as evidence of the existence of an original.

In certain circumstances your will can be changed, the Courts may agree to alter the bequests made in it if they are challenged. You will may also be revoked if it is not correctly signed or witnessed or does not comply with any other legal requirements.

Challenges

Whilst in theory you can leave what you like to whom you wish, this is not quite true in practice. You would be expected to leave adequate provision to your spouse and any dependent children, for example. If anyone believes that they are entitled to more than they have been bequeathed, they can challenge the will in the Courts.

If a man dies and leaves £5,000 to his wife and £100,000 to a donkey sanctuary, she is quite entitled to challenge the will and is likely to receive sympathy from the Courts.

Although anyone may challenge a will, it is normally confined to the following:

- Spouse – can make a full claim.
- Ex-spouse – can claim for maintenance, particularly if he or she is receiving alimony payments. The exception is if the divorce or legal separation took place within one year of death then a full claim can be made.
- Children – can claim for maintenance, especially if dependent upon the decreased at the time of death.
- Step-children – as for children.
- Other dependents – anyone who was being supported by the deceased at the time of death, such as a common law partner or an aged parent.

Conditions

It is quite acceptable to place conditions on the beneficiaries before they can inherit. Examples are that the spouse must not remarry for a defined but reasonable period of time after the death; children and/or grandchildren must reach a certain age before they can inherit; the money can only be used to pay for a university education and so on.

However, some conditions may be considered 'unreasonable' and can be challenged in the Courts. If the Courts agree with the challenger, the beneficiary will inherit without complying with the condition.

Each challenge is judged on the facts and circumstances and in most instances the following would be considered to be 'unreasonable':

- Not to marry or remarry – except in the case mentioned above, this would be unreasonable.
- Remain celibate – unless the person was already practising celibacy, such as a Roman Catholic priest, this would not be considered acceptable.
- Inducing the break-up of a marriage – if the condition was that the beneficiary should divorce his/her partner within say three years, it would be rendered void.
- Separating children from parents – it is not acceptable to impose a condition that a child is separated from one or both parents.
- Performing a criminal act – any condition which entails the person to break the law would be unreasonable and voided.
- Religious practice – it would be considered unreasonable to impose a condition making the beneficiary convert to another religion or sect.

It is therefore advisable to consult a solicitor before imposing conditions in your will to ensure that they are acceptable.

 KEEPING YOUR AFFAIRS IN ORDER

To help your executors to administer your estate after your death, it is vitally important that **they know where to find all the documents and relevant information relating to your estate**. List all documents together with where they are kept. Whilst many items will be at home, others such as share certificates may be with your bank.

Below is a checklist of documents and information that your executors will need.

Documents	Information
• your will	• National Insurance
• birth certificate	number
• marriage certificate	• place of work
• divorce papers	• solicitor
• passport	• accountant
• driving licence	• insurance broker
• bank accounts	• tax number
• building society accounts	• tax office
• post office accounts	• list of valuables
• pension book	• money owed.
• insurance policies	
• share certificates	
• Premium Bonds	
• hire purchase/rental agreements	
• unpaid bills.	

MAKING WHAT MATTERS WORK FOR YOU

✓ Remember to make sufficient provisions for your dependants, to avoid your will being challenged.

✓ Own your property in joint tenancy with your spouse, and have joint accounts, and this will save tax and make life easier for those you leave behind.

✓ Plan your will carefully, decide what you want to leave to whom. Avoid imposing conditions which may be deemed 'unreasonable'. Make sure that your will is signed, dated and witnessed correctly. Appoint executors who are willing and able to act on your behalf.

✓ Use a solicitor to make your will to ensure clarity and validity.

✓ Check your will at regular intervals. Ensure that your executors know where to find your will and other documents and information.

Useful Addresses

GENERAL

Age Concern, Astral House, 1268 London Road, London SW16 4ER. Tel: (020) 8765 7200.

Age Concern Scotland, 113 Rose Street, Edinburgh EH2 3DT. Tel: (0131) 220 3345.

Age Concern Cymru, 4th Floor, 1 Cathedral Road, Cardiff CF1 9SD. Tel: (029) 2037 1566.

Age Concern Northern Ireland, 3 Lower Crescent, Belfast BT7 1NR. Tel: (028) 9024 5729.

Help the Aged, St James's Walk, Clerkenwell Green, London EC1R 0BE. Tel: (020) 7253 0253.

FINANCE

Independent Financial Adviser Promotion, 17–19 Emery Road, Bristol BS4 5PF. Tel: (0117) 971 1177.

Financial Services Authority, 25 North Colonnade, Canary Wharf, London E14 5HS. Tel: (020) 7676 1000.

Money Management Council, PO Box 77, Hertford, Herts SG14 2HW. Tel: (01992) 503448.

EDUCATION

The Open University, PO Box 625, Walton Hall, Milton Keynes MK7 6AA. Tel: (01908) 858585.

The University of the Third Age, 26 Harrison Street, London WC1H 8JG. Tel: (020) 7837 8838.

Open College of Arts, Houndhill, Worsborough, Barnsley S70 6TU. Tel: (01226) 730495.

National Extension College, 18 Brooklands Avenue, Cambridge CB2 2HN. Tel: (01223) 316644.

The National Institute of Adult Continuing Education, 21 De

Montfort Street, Leicester LE1 7GE. Tel: (01162) 551451.

WORK AND SELF-EMPLOYMENT

Third Age Challenge Limited, Anglia House, 115 Commercial Road, Swindon SN1 5PL. Tel: (01793) 533370.

New Ways to Work, 309 Upper Street, London N1 2TY. Tel: (020) 7226 4026.

The Careers and Occupational Information Centre, PO Box 298A, Thames Ditton, Surrey KT7 O25. Tel: (020) 8957 5030.

Training and Enterprise Councils. Tel: (0800) 100 900.

LEISURE AND HOLIDAYS

SAGA, Resort Operations Department, The Saga Building, Middleburgh Square, Folkestone, Kent CT20 1AZ. Tel: (01303) 711111.

Eurocamp, Overseas Recruitment Department, Canute Court, Toft Road, Knutsford, Cheshire WA16 ONL. Tel: (01565) 625522.

Travel Companions, 12 Portland Place, Leamingon Spa, Warks CV32 5EU. Tel: (01926) 332911.

The Cinnamon Trust, Foundry House, Foundry Square, Hayle, Cornwall TR27 4HH. Tel: (01736) 757900.

Oral History Society, Department of Sociology, University of Essex, Wivenhoe Park, Colchester CO4 2SQ. Tel: (020) 7412 7405.

Federation of Family History Societies, The Benson Room, Birmingham and Midland Institute, Margaret Street, Birmingham B3 3BS.

The Running Sixties, 120 Norfolk Avenue, Sanderstead, Surrey CR2 8BS. Tel: (020) 8657 7660.

The Ugly Model Agency, Tigres House, 256 Edgware Road,

London W2 1DS. Tel: (020) 7402 5564.

National Gardens Scheme, Hatchlands Park, East Clandon, Guildford, Surrey GU4 7RT. Tel: (01483) 211535.

BBC Ticket Unit, BBC Television Audience Services, Wood Lane, Shepherd's Bush, London W12 7RJ.

The Ticket Unit, BBC Radio, Broadcasting House, London W1A 1AA.

VOLUNTEERING

The National Centre for Volunteering, Regent's Wharf, 8 All Saints Street, London N1 9RL. Tel: (020) 7520 8900.

British Trust for Conservation Volunteers, 36 St Mary's Street, Wallingford, Oxon OX10 0EU. Tel: (01491) 839766.

Wildlife Trusts, The Green, Witham Park, Waterside, South Lincoln LN5 7RJ. Tel: (01522) 544400.

Community Service Volunteers, 237 Pentonville Road, Lodon N1 9NJ. Tel: (020) 7278 6601.